MY SPORT

AMERICAN FOOTBALL

Tim Wood

Photographs: Chris Fairclough

Franklin Watts
London • New York • Sydney • Toronto

© 1989 Franklin Watts

Franklin Watts
12a Golden Square
London W1R 4BA

Phototypeset by Lineage, Watford
Printed in Italy by G. Canale & C. S.p.A. - Turin
Design: K and Co

UK ISBN: 0 86313 824 1

The publishers, author and photographer would like to thank Cyril Stewart, Robert Alley and the players of the Heathrow Jets American Football Club for their help and co-operation in the production of this book.

The footballer featured in this book is Cyril Stewart. He plays running back for the Heathrow Jets. Cyril was a good games player at school, though not a particularly fast runner. He became interested in American Football through watching it on TV, and joined the Fulham Cardinals American Football Club soon after leaving school. Recently he moved to the Jets. He does regular weight training and fitness exercises, and trains with the team at least twice a week. Cyril works in a dry cleaners.

I am an American Footballer. Today my team has a home game. I arrive at the ground about three hours before the game starts, and begin my warm-up routine.

Before the game begins, each player has his ankles taped. The strips of sticky tape are wound in several directions.

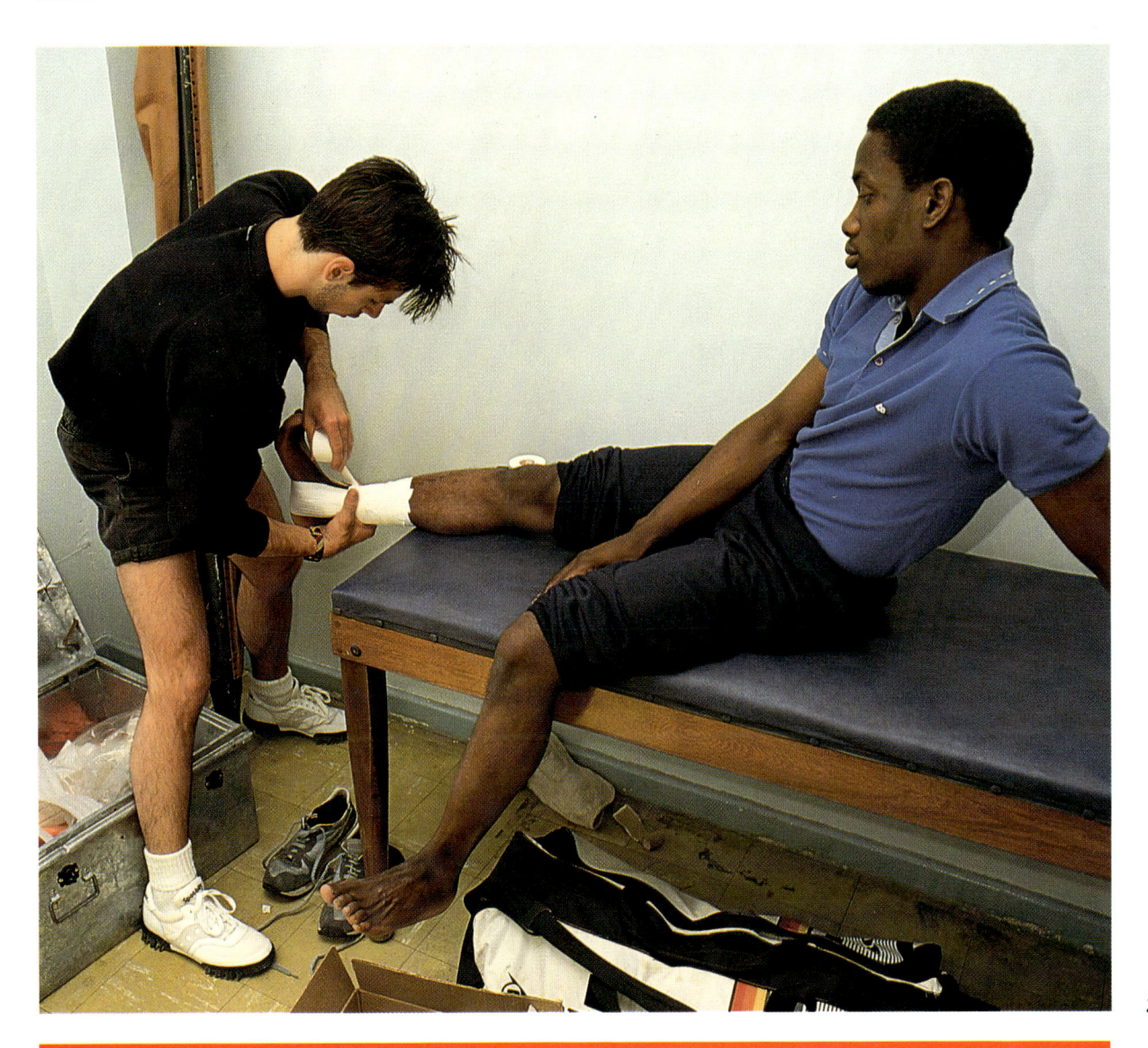

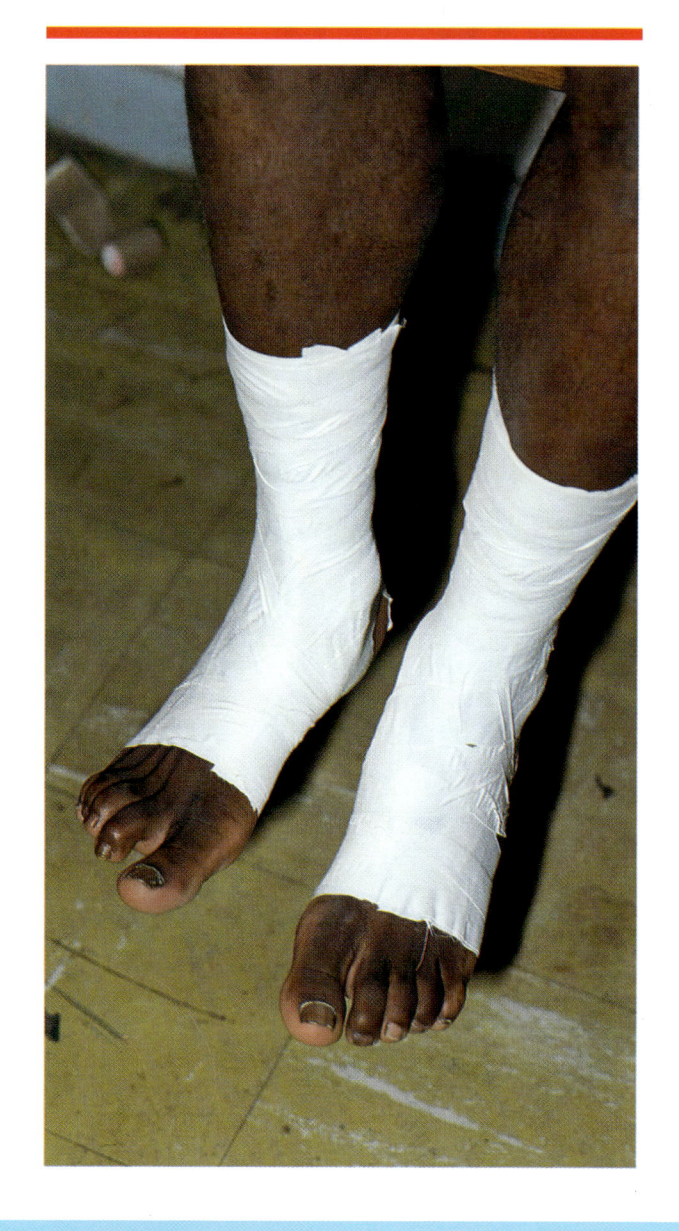

The sticky tape holds the ankles rigid. This stops them from twisting or bending during the game, and prevents many injuries.

This is my football kit. The plastic pads protect my body and legs from injury during the game.

My football helmet is lined with plastic air bags. These are inflated with a special pump to make the helmet fit my head perfectly.

Before the game, the team's kit is laid out in the changing room. The trousers have special pockets to hold the plastic pads.

9

Each player wears plastic body armour. It is quite light but extremely strong. It protects the player's shoulders and upper body.

Before the game begins, the whole team does warm-up exercises. This puts us in the right mood to play and also prepares our muscles and joints for the hard game to come.

11

Each team has many different attacking moves or 'plays'. A play starts with a 'snap', when the centre passes the ball through his legs to the quarterback. Before the game, the offensive linemen practise several snaps.

12

The linemen practise charging. This warms them up and puts them in the right mood to play an attacking game.

More about the game

A game of American Football lasts one hour of actual play. This is split into four quarters. A team's attacking side is called the offence. Its defending side is called the defence. There are 45 players in an American Football team, but only 11 are allowed on to the field for a play.

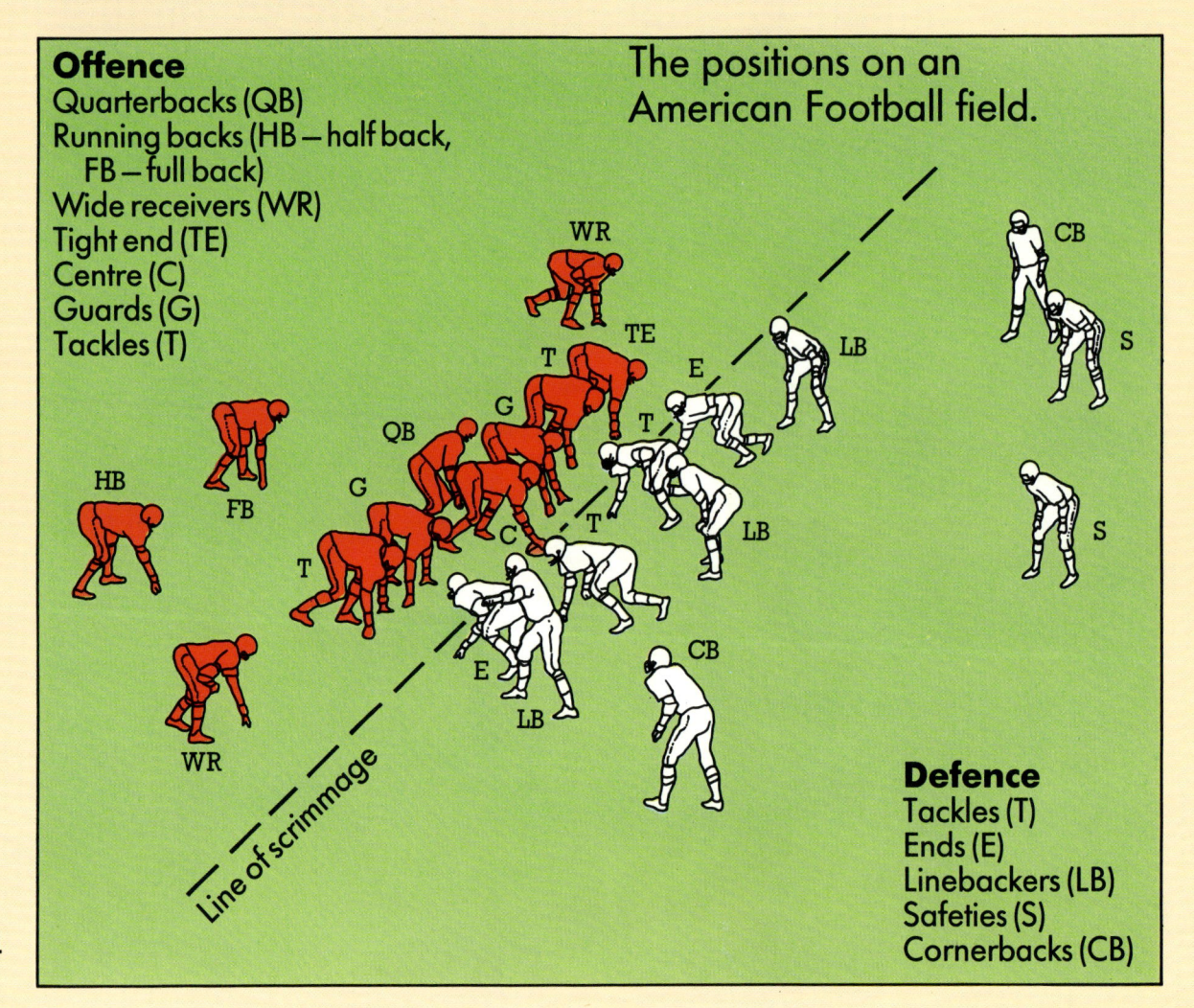

Offence
Quarterbacks (QB)
Running backs (HB – half back, FB – full back)
Wide receivers (WR)
Tight end (TE)
Centre (C)
Guards (G)
Tackles (T)

The positions on an American Football field.

Line of scrimmage

Defence
Tackles (T)
Ends (E)
Linebackers (LB)
Safeties (S)
Cornerbacks (CB)

Ball
21 1/4 in (54 cm)
11 in (28 cm)

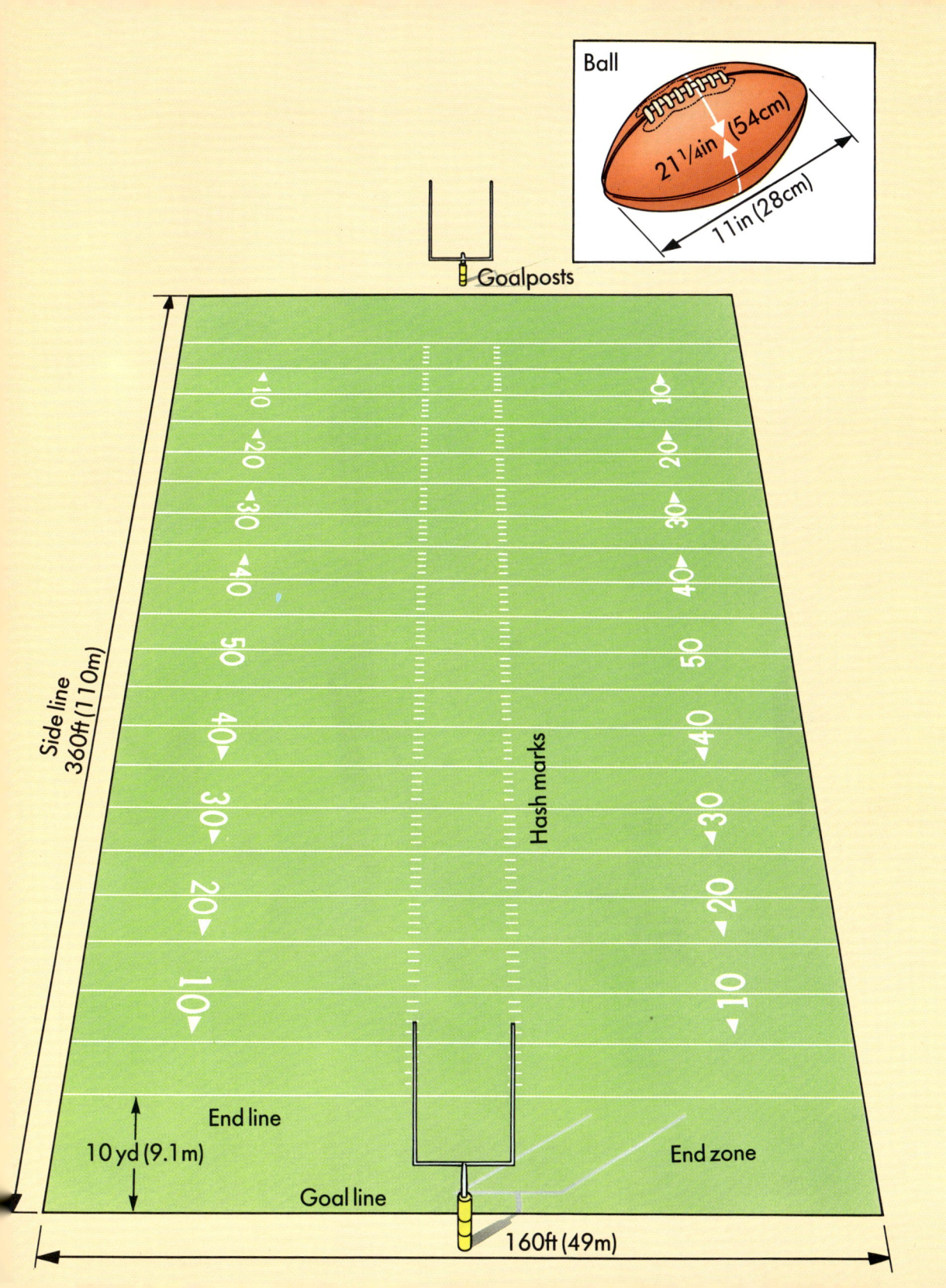

Goalposts

Side line 360 ft (110 m)

Hash marks

End line
10 yd (9.1 m)
Goal line
End zone
160 ft (49 m)

15

The running backs and wide receivers try out some of their plays to get used to handling the ball and to make sure they are quite fit.

I practise one of my plays. I run behind a blocker while another player protects my right side.

17

The game starts with a kick-off. The kicker tries to send the ball deep into the opponents' half.

There are seven officials who control the game. They throw yellow flags on to the ground if there is a foul. They use special hand signals and radios to announce their decisions.

19

The offence have four attempts to move the ball 10 yards (9 metres). The umpires use a chain to check how far they have taken it.

While our offence are on the field, our defence watch from the sidelines.

The cheerleaders dance and sing to encourage the Jets. They practise for four hours each week and come with us to all our games.

Before making a play, the offensive team goes into a huddle. During the huddle, the quarterback tells the team which play will be used.

Each play has a different code number which each member of the team must learn off by heart. Each player must know exactly what to do and where to run during all the plays.

When the play has been chosen, the players take their positions. The two rows of linemen crouch down and face each other at the line of scrimmage.

When the ball is snapped back, the Jets' linemen try to protect their quarterback from the opponents' linemen who try to 'sack' him.

The quarterback passes the ball to me. I manage to wriggle through the tacklers, helped by a team-mate who acts as a blocker.

I run very fast to make as many yards as possible before I am tackled.

During this tackle, I am injured. The physiotherapist puts an ice pack on my strained ankle. I cannot continue. I watch the rest of the game from the sidelines. I am very happy when Jets eventually win.

FACTS ABOUT AMERICAN FOOTBALL

The inventor of American football was Walter Camp. He was a student at Yale University in the 1870s who adapted rules from rugby and soccer to produce the modern game.

Early games led to many injuries. In the 1905 season eighteen players were killed and 159 seriously injured. President Theodore Roosevelt ordered the rules to be changed to make the game safer.

Professional footballers made their first appearance in the 1890s.

The National Football League (NFL) was organised into two 'conferences', the American Football Conference (AFC) and the National Football Conference (NFC) in 1970. The champions of each conference play in the Super Bowl.

The longest game ever played was on Christmas Day, 1971, when the game between the Miami Dolphins and the Kansas City Chiefs went 22 minutes and 40 seconds into overtime. The total playing time was 82 minutes 40 seconds. Miami won 27-24.

The most points scored in a football career was 2002 by George Blanda (1949-75).

The most yards gained by rushing in a football career was 17,726 by Walter Payton (1975-88).

The highest number of pass receptions in a career was 759 by Steve Largent (1975-88).

GLOSSARY

Blocking
The deliberate and legal obstruction of an attacking opponent who does not have the ball.

Down
A unit of play. Each time the player carrying the ball is tackled and brought to the ground, play stops. It is restarted with a set piece called a down.

End zone
The area at either end of the field where 'touchdowns' are scored.

Line of scrimmage
The place where the ball is grounded at the end of a play and where the game restarts for the next play.

Physiotherapist
An expert at treating sports injuries.

Play
An attacking move made by the offense.

Rushing
A method of moving the ball forward in which the quarterback gives the ball to a player who runs with it in order to gain ground.

Sack
When the quarterback is caught in possession of the ball, behind the line of scrimmage, before he can pass it.

Touchdown
Awarded when a player from the offense either catches the ball in the end zone or runs with the ball into the end zone. It is worth 6 points. After scoring a touchdown, the successful side can score an extra point by kicking the ball through the goalposts.

Index

Body armour 10
Block 31
Blocker 17, 27

Chain 20
Changing room 9
Cheerleaders 22

Defence 14, 21, 29
Down 29

End zone 14, 29

Foul 19

Hand signals 19

Helmet 8
Huddle 23, 29

Injury 6, 7, 27, 29

Kicker 18
Kick-off 18
Kit 7, 9, 28
Linemen 12, 13, 25, 26

Offence 14, 20, 21, 23, 29, 30

Pads 7, 9
Passing 12, 27, 29
Physiotherapist 27, 29
Play 12, 14, 16, 17, 23, 24, 25, 27, 29

Quarterback 12, 14, 23, 26, 27, 29

Running back 3, 14, 16
Rushing 29

Sack 26, 29
Scrimmage 14, 25, 29
Snap 12, 26, 29

Tackle 27, 28, 29
Tape 5, 6
Touchdown 29

Umpire 20

Warm-up 4, 11, 13
Wide receiver 16